IMAGES
of America

FORT LARAMIE

IMAGES
of America

FORT LARAMIE

Starley Talbott

ARCADIA
PUBLISHING

Published by Arcadia Publishing
Charleston, South Carolina

Printed in the United States of America

Library of Congress Control Number: 2009939080

For all general information contact Arcadia Publishing at:
Telephone 843-853-2070
Fax 843-853-0044
E-mail sales@arcadiapublishing.com
For customer service and orders:
Toll-Free 1-888-313-2665

Visit us on the Internet at www.arcadiapublishing.com

To my grandchildren,
that they may be lovers of history
and explorers of their world.

CONTENTS

ACKNOWLEDGMENTS

The staff and volunteers at the Fort Laramie National Historic Site provided immeasurable assistance in assembling this book. Special thanks go to Mitzi Frank, superintendent, and Baird Todd, museum specialist. I am grateful to Baird Todd for his very helpful suggestions. My utmost appreciation goes to Sandra Lowry, librarian, for her hours of searching photographic files and her cheerful attitude. I also thank the staff at the Wyoming State Archives, Department of Parks and Cultural Resources, especially Suzi Taylor, reference archivist, and Robin Everett, receptionist. Most of the photographs are from the collection at the Fort Laramie National Historic Site and will be identified by FLNHS. I also wish to thank my editor at Arcadia Publishing, Sabrina Heise, for her support and guidance and my husband, Beauford Thompson, for his encouragement.

INTRODUCTION

From the time of its founding, Fort Laramie has served like a grand meeting hall for both nature and humankind: where the mountains meet the plains; where two rivers converge; where Native American tribes gathered; where fur trappers and traders rendezvoused; where emigrants met for rest and supplies; where soldiers came and went; where homesteaders linked the past to the present; and where today's travelers come to partake in Fort Laramie's fascinating history.

As America expanded westward, this outpost in the Wyoming wilderness was crucial to the transformation of the West. From its 1834 founding as a trading post, initially called Fort William, to its abandonment by the army in 1890, the fort played a significant role in the settling of the West. Fort Laramie was involved in the fur and buffalo hide trade, overland migrations, Native American wars and treaties, Civil War maneuvering, and the establishment of the telegraph, pony express, and railroad.

The list of characters who passed through Fort Laramie, the crossroads of the American West, included mountain men, Native Americans, soldiers, explorers, religious leaders, and emigrants. Robert Stuart, the first known white person to visit the site that would become Fort Laramie, camped with companions at the mouth of the Laramie River on December 22, 1812. Jedediah Smith and Thomas Fitzpatrick led an expedition into the area in 1823. Alfred Jacob Miller, on an expedition in 1837, became the first artist to record the Fort Laramie landscape.

Religious leaders who visited the fort included Dr. Marcus Whitman; his wife, Narcissa; Rev. Henry Spaulding; his wife, Elizabeth; and members of a missionary party that traveled west in 1836. Narcissa and Elizabeth were the first white women to visit Fort Laramie. Fr. Pierre Jean DeSmet visited Fort Laramie on June 4, 1840, and he returned in 1851 to attend the treaty council. Brigham Young led the first group of Mormons west, stopping in Fort Laramie on June 1, 1847.

Noteworthy Native Americans in the history of Fort Laramie included Spotted Tail, chief of the Brule Sioux, and Red Cloud, chief of the Oglala Sioux.

Many military men left their marks on Fort Laramie, both good and bad. Col. Henry Carrington, Lt. Caspar Collins, Col. Thomas Moonlight, Gen. William Sherman, Gen. Phillip Sheridan, and Gen. George Crook, among many others, were influential leaders.

Other noteworthy Western characters to visit Fort Laramie included Wild Bill Hickok, Mark Twain, Wyatt Earp, and Buffalo Bill Cody. A woman of note was Martha Jane Cannary (Calamity Jane), who frequented the Fort Laramie area. Her exploits are legendary, including the time she disguised herself as one of the cavalry troopers escorting an expedition. When she was later discovered masquerading as one of General Crook's muleskinners, she was placed under arrest and sent packing back to Fort Laramie.

Beginning in 1841, emigrants bound for the West Coast stopped in Fort Laramie as they traveled what would become the Oregon, California, and Mormon Trails. This westward migration peaked in the early 1850s at more than 50,000 people traveling the trails annually.

The U.S. military purchased the post in 1849, and soldiers were stationed there to protect the wagon trains. Fort Laramie had served as a social and economic center for thousands of Native Americans, but the amicable relationship between the fort and the natives gradually deteriorated into one of dependency, resentment, and, finally, hostility.

Early in 1851, Congress had authorized a great treaty council with the Plains Indians to assure peaceful relations along the trails to the west. Fort Laramie was chosen as the meeting place, and various Native American tribes were invited to converge at the site. By September 1, thousands of natives and their ponies had arrived. The horses required so much forage that the vast assemblage had to move to the meadows at the mouth of Horse Creek, 30 miles east of the fort. Speeches ensued, gifts were distributed, and the peace pipe was smoked. By September 17, it had been agreed that peace should reign among the Native Americans and the newcomers. The emigrants were to be free to travel the roads and hold their scattered forts, and the natives were to receive an annuity of $50,000 in goods each year. The council was considered a great success and gave promise of lasting peace on the plains. The ink was hardly dry on the treaty before trouble began.

The Grattan and Harney Massacres marred the relations with Native Americans and whites from 1854 to 1855. Whites continued to trespass on lands the natives considered their habitat, and Native Americans continued to commit depredations along the trails.

The outbreak of the Civil War led to the reduction of garrisons at all outposts. This, coupled with a bloody uprising of the Sioux in Minnesota in 1862, inspired the Plains Indians to go on the warpath. Incidents provoked by both whites and natives continued to plague efforts to maintain peace. Termination of the Civil War in 1865 released many troops for service against the Native Americans.

Natives' resentment intensified in the 1860s as hundreds of wagons rolled over the Bozeman Trail through Sioux hunting grounds on their way to the gold and silver fields of Montana. The army angered the more moderate Native Americans like Sioux leader Red Cloud by building Forts Reno, Phil Kearny, and C. F. Smith along the Bozeman Trail. The Native Americans responded with attacks on travelers and soldiers. The Fetterman, Hayfield, and Wagon Box Fights were major actions of Red Cloud's War of 1866 to 1868.

After several unsuccessful attempts to arrange peace councils, the peace commissioners came again to Fort Laramie in April and May 1868. They signed separate treaties with the Arapaho and Cheyenne Indians; the Crow Indians; and the Sioux Indians. They were prepared to grant the Sioux demands, including abandonment of the Bozeman Trail, called for by Chief Red Cloud. By late May, both the Brule and Oglala Sioux had signed the treaty, but Red Cloud refused to sign until the troops had left the Power River country and his warriors had burned the abandoned Fort Phil Kearny to the ground. Later that year, Red Cloud came to Fort Laramie and signed the treaty.

The Fort Laramie Treaty of 1868 did not end the fighting. Its terms were broken when gold was discovered in 1874 in the Black Hills, a sacred area well inside lands guaranteed to the Sioux by the treaty. The Great Sioux Campaign of 1876 followed, with Fort Laramie serving as a major staging and logistical center. Fort Laramie remained an important supply and communications center during the years the army was slowly forcing the Northern Plains Indians onto reservations. Most Native Americans were finally confined to reservations by 1877. With the end of native hostilities, the fort declined in importance and was eventually closed.

After Fort Laramie was abandoned by the military in 1890, all but one of the fort's 60 structures were sold at public auction. The buildings were used as private dwellings, businesses, a dance hall, and livestock shelters during the fort's homestead period from 1890 to 1937. Many buildings were stripped of usable lumber and left to deteriorate.

Because of the interest of a few homesteaders, local residents, and others, efforts to preserve the fort began in the 1930s. Fort Laramie was acquired by the State of Wyoming in 1937 and became a unit of the national park system in 1938. Today Fort Laramie National Historic Site is open daily to the public, except New Year's Day, Thanksgiving, and Christmas. The restoration of many structures to their historic appearance provides visitors with a glimpse of a bygone era. Buildings are outfitted with authentic furnishings, and costumed interpreters often present historical tours and vignettes. Fort Laramie continues to serve as a grand meeting hall where the Great Plains meet the Rocky Mountains in southeastern Wyoming.

One

THE TRAPPERS, TRADERS, AND EARLY EMIGRANTS

This view of Fort William in 1837 is from a sketch by A. J. Miller, an artist who accompanied Sir William Drummond Stewart to the mountains in 1837. Fur traders William Sublette and Robert Campbell had established the log fort in 1834 near the confluence of the Laramie and North Platte Rivers. They sold their fort in 1835 to Jim Bridger, Thomas Fitzpatrick, and Milton Sublette, who in turn sold it to the American Fur Company in 1836. The fort served as the supply base for the traders and was loaded with trade goods brought to the fort by annual supply caravans. (Courtesy of the Wyoming State Archives, Department of State Parks and Cultural Resources.)

This image shows the interior of Fort William from an 1837 drawing by A. J. Miller. Miller's notes describe the fort as being "of a quadrangular form with block houses at diagonal corners to sweep the fronts in case of attack . . . the Indians encamp in great numbers here 3 or 4 times a year, bringing peltries to be exchanged for dry goods, tobacco, beads and alcohol." (Courtesy of the Wyoming State Archives, Department of State Parks and Cultural Resources.)

The rival adobe-walled Fort Platte, only 1 mile away, and the eventual deterioration of Fort William prompted the American Fur Company to replace it in 1841 with an adobe-walled post. The new fort was located near a bend of the Laramie River, presumably up river from the old fort (though the exact location of old Fort William has never been determined). They named the new facility Fort John, but like its predecessor, it was popularly known as Fort Laramie. This photograph shows an imaginative view of Fort John in 1849. (Courtesy of FLNHS, from the Signal Corps collection.)

Early traders traveled to the mountains to meet the fur trappers at the summer rendezvous. The traders bartered with the mountain men for beaver pelts and other furs. This photograph shows an artist's rendition of the traditional American trapper. One early trapper, Jacques La Ramee, of who little is known, left his mark forever on the area of southeastern Wyoming. The adaptation of his name to Laramie became the name of a town, a county, a mountain peak, a river, and a fort. (Courtesy of FLNHS, from the National Park Service collection.)

Abandonment of the rendezvous system after 1840 increased the importance of fixed trading posts. The trappers then relied on their own means of transportation to bring their furs to the post for trading. Both trappers and traders came to be more and more dependent upon Fort Laramie as a base for supplies and as a refuge. This photograph shows an artist's rendition of a trapper's pack train. (Courtesy of FLNHS, from the National Park Service collection.)

By around 1840, many of the beaver had been trapped out, and silk hats were replacing hats made from beaver. Buffalo robes became the prime trading commodity at Fort Laramie. Both trappers and Native Americans came to the fort to trade buffalo hides. This photograph shows an artist's rendition of a buffalo hunt. (Courtesy of Scotts Bluff National Monument, from the FLNHS collection.)

This photograph is a copy of a painting by William Henry Jackson of the Smith-Jackson-Sublette wagon train in 1830. This was the first wagon train to follow the Oregon, California, or Mormon Trail. By the 1840s, thousands of emigrants began crossing the plains bound for free land in Oregon and California. Mormons came seeking religious freedom, and after 1848, miners sought gold in California. This westward migration peaked in the 1850s at more than 50,000 immigrants each year. (Courtesy of Scotts Bluff National Monument, from the FLNHS collection.)

Wagon trains reached approximately the halfway point of the arduous journey from Independence, Missouri, to the West Coast when they reached Fort Laramie. This photograph shows an artist's rendition of covered wagons fording the Platte River. (Courtesy of Scotts Bluff National Monument, from the FLNHS collection.)

The Mormons began migrating to Utah in the 1840s to escape religious bigotry in the eastern states. One of their leaders was Brigham Young, who led the first group of Mormons to their Zion, the valley of the Great Salt Lake in 1847. Young and this first group of pioneers camped near Fort Laramie on June 1, 1847. Brigham Young conceived and implemented the handcart system in 1856, whereby Mormon emigrants began passing through Fort Laramie walking and pulling handcarts to carry their goods across the country. (Courtesy of FLNHS.)

Buffalo hides, such as the one in this photograph, were the main item of trade at Fort Laramie after the beaver had mostly been trapped out. The above photograph was taken by the author at a re-creation of a trapper's camp during the 175th anniversary celebration of Fort William at Fort Laramie in 2009. (Courtesy of the author.)

This photograph shows a typical trapper's tent with equipment the trapper would have used when acquiring furs for trade. The photograph was taken by the author during the 175th anniversary celebration of Fort William at Fort Laramie in 2009. Living history demonstrators recreated the 1834 camp of William Sublette, fur trader and founder of Fort William. (Courtesy of the author.)

Two

THE MILITARY, NATIVES, TREATIES, AND EMIGRANTS

In the earliest known photograph of Fort Laramie, taken in 1858, the remains of old Fort John can be seen in the left middle ground. Directly behind it are three officers' quarters, constructed in 1850. Old Bedlam, the legendary white two-story officers' quarters, dominates the center of the view. Other structures are barely visible in this photograph, which accompanied William Lee's manuscript diary of 1858. (Courtesy of the Library of Congress, from the FLNHS collection.)

9. FORT LARAMIE.

The U.S. Army built a string of outposts along the immigrant trails to protect the travelers from increasing conflicts with Native Americans. Fort Laramie was purchased by the army in 1849 for $4,000. The army laid out a new post around a large parade ground with stables, a bakery, and officers' and soldiers' quarters. William Henry Jackson took this 1870 photograph of Fort Laramie, showing

numerous new buildings constructed to support a base for military operations and a distribution point for Native American annuities. (Courtesy of the Wyoming State Archives, Department of State Parks and Cultural Resources, from the United States Geological Survey collection.)

Jim Bridger was a famed mountain man, trapper, and a frequent visitor to Fort Laramie. He was also sought after as a competent guide by emigrants and military alike. In his later years, Bridger spent many hours at Fort Laramie. He stayed in a room at the Post Trader's Store, where he recounted, sometimes exaggerated, stories of his life adventures. (Courtesy of FLNHS.)

Gen. William Harney intended to punish the Sioux Indians for the event known as the Grattan Massacre, which occurred near Fort Laramie in 1854. Harney led troops against the Sioux, culminating in the Battle of Blue Water Creek on September 2, 1855. They attacked the village, killing 86 Native Americans and capturing women and children. General Harney issued a stern warning to other Sioux bands, before proceeding to Fort Pierre. General Harney later served with the peace commission during the 1868 Fort Laramie Treaty. (Courtesy of FLNHS.)

This photograph was taken in 1938, long after an unfortunate event occurred here. This was the site of the incident known as the Grattan Massacre in 1854. Until August 18, 1854, immigrants had passed through the country near Fort Laramie with little trouble from Native Americans. A tribe of Brule Sioux was camped about 8 miles east of Fort Laramie. As a Mormon caravan passed the village, a cow strayed into the camp, where it was promptly killed and butchered by a visiting Miniconjou. The Mormons reported the theft on their arrival at Fort Laramie. Brevet 2nd Lt. John Grattan, 6th Infantry, with 29 soldiers, 2 cannons, and a drunken interpreter, was dispatched to the village to arrest the offending Native American. A fight erupted when the Miniconjou brave refused to give himself up. The Sioux chief Conquering Bear was killed, and the entire military party was annihilated. Even though the enraged Sioux threatened a further attack on Fort Laramie, they did not follow through and moved out of the area. (Courtesy of FLNHS.)

Col. William G. Bullock (shown at left) was the partner of Seth Ward, the post sutler (trader). During the military occupation of Fort Laramie, a post sutler was licensed by the government to operate a store for the benefit of the soldiers and civilians. The sutler was granted the exclusive right to trade on the military reservation in exchange for having his prices fixed by a board of officers and for paying a head-tax according to the average number of troops. (Courtesy of FLNHS.)

This photograph, by the famous photographer William Henry Jackson, shows how the Sutler's Store looked in 1877. The unidentified people in the photograph are ranchers, farmers, freighters, and cattlemen, who traded at Sutler's Store in Fort Laramie. (Courtesy of FLNHS.)

Seth Ward was the sutler at Fort Laramie from 1857 to 1871. Margaret Carrington, the wife of Col. Henry Carrington, described the store. "The long counter of Mssrs. Bullock and Ward was a scene of seeming confusion. . . . Indians mingled with soldiers of the garrison, teamsters, emigrants, speculators, half-breeds and interpreters. Cups of rice, sugar, coffee, or flour . . . along with brilliant calicoes, and flashing ribbons passed over the same counter with knives and tobacco, brass nails and glass beads." (Courtesy of the Native Sons and Daughters of Greater Kansas City, from the FLNHS collection.)

This photograph by the author shows the interior of Sutler's Store as it is today. The store is furnished with authentic articles like those that would have been for sale in the store around 1865. A buffalo robe sits on the counter top. (Courtesy of the author.)

The single most recognizable building at Fort Laramie is the bachelor officers' quarters, nicknamed Old Bedlam. It is pictured here as it looked around 1875. It was the first building erected by the army after it took over the post in 1849. The building gained a reputation for wild parties by the officers residing there, thus acquiring the nickname of Old Bedlam. By the mid-1870s, a coat of dark red paint had been applied to Old Bedlam's exterior, detracting from its former white splendor. (Courtesy of the FLNHS.)

Officers are shown at Fort Laramie in 1888. Among those pictured are Capt. Thomas Traxell, 17th Infantry; Capt. Charles Parker, 9th Infantry; Capt. Clarence Bailey, 8th Infantry; a Colonel Mizner, 17th Infantry; Col. Henry Morrow, 21st Infantry; Capt. Augustus Corliss, 8th Infantry; a Captain Beuhave, 6th Infantry; a Captain Cleadware, 9th Cavalry; Capt. William Worth, 8th Infantry; Capt. Clarence Bennett, 17th Infantry; Lt. Col. John Poland, 21st Infantry; Capt. Cyrus Roberts, 17th Infantry; Capt. Frederick Ebstieu, 21st Infantry; and Lt. Col. Robert Offley, 17th Infantry. (Courtesy of FLNHS.)

No I; Church Howe U S
          Marshall Ter. Wyo:
No 2 ;Indian Com. Bennett
No 3 ;Indian Com Campbell
No 4; Major Crittenden
          5th U S Cavelry
No 5   General Flint
No 6   O N Unthank U.S .
          Telegraph operator
No 7; Rev A Wright
          Post Chaplin
Other Luit's Cox, Webster
Ezikal ,Captian O'Connor
and Major Powell.
8- Major Powell.

Officers and civilians posed on the front porch of Old Bedlam around 1870. Among those pictured are Church Howe, U.S. Marshall, Wyoming Territory; ? Bennett, Indian commissioner; Robert Campbell, Indian commissioner; a Major Crittenden, 5th Cavalry; Gen. Franklin Flint; Oliver Uthank, telegraph operator; Rev. A. Wright, post chaplain; a Lieutenant Cox; a Lieutenant Webster; a Lieutenant Erikal; a Captain O'Connor; and Maj. James Powell. The others are unidentified. (Courtesy of the FLNHS.)

Oliver Uthank was a telegrapher at Fort Laramie from 1869 to 1874. The telegraph operator was considered a favored job in the military. Pvt. Hervey Johnson wrote in his diary that he wished he had taken the time to learn the trade. Johnson said telegraph operators earned $60 per month from the telegraph company, besides their government pay, rations, and clothing, and they had no military duties to perform. (Courtesy of the FLNHS.)

As a result of the 1849 Gold Rush to California, the 1847 Mormon exodus to Utah, and the thousands of others who moved west, the need for a fast mail service beyond the Rocky Mountains was a necessity. The Butterfield Overland Mail Service in the South and private carriers filled some of the need, but a more central mail route was needed. The formation of the Leavenworth and Pike's Peak Express Company by William H. Russell, Alexander Major, and William B. Waddell provided the new route, which became known as the Pony Express. It operated from April 1860 to October 1861, covering more than 1,800 miles in 10 days from St. Joseph, Missouri, to Sacramento, California. Young men aboard fast horses each rode segments ranging from 65 to 100 miles, stopping at relay stations along the way. This photograph is an artist's rendition of a Pony Express rider waving as he sped away. Shown in the background is the construction of telegraph lines, which soon replaced the Pony Express. (Courtesy of Scotts Bluff National Monument, from the FLNHS collection.)

Col. William "Buffalo Bill" Cody was a Pony Express rider, buffalo hunter, scout, and showman. Cody became a Pony Express rider at age 15, and he claimed to have performed a famous ride. Cody arrived at a relay station to find the relief rider dead, whereupon he mounted a fresh horse, rode to the next station, and made the return ride, covering a distance of around 325 miles. (Courtesy of Wyoming State Archives, Department of State Parks and Cultural Resources.)

This photograph was taken from a drawing of an unidentified Pony Express station around 1860. The mail was carried in a pouch called a *mochila*, a leather-covered device that fit over the saddle frame. At each station the incoming rider jumped off his horse, pulled the *mochila* off, and transferred it to the next horse and rider to continue on its way. (Courtesy of Wyoming State Archives, Department of State Parks and Cultural Resources.)

Soldiers are shown at drill practice in this photograph from around 1884. Soldiers were assigned to Fort Laramie to protect immigrants along the Oregon Trail, but actual combat was rare, and most soldiers never saw a hostile Native American. A rigid routine of drill and fatigue duties set the tone for most of the soldier's days. An officer's life was less regimented than the enlisted men, and some officers reported that the daily routine was "rather monotonous." (Courtesy of the FLNHS.)

Soldiers are shown at ease by their tents in this photograph from around 1884. The frontier army contained a number of recent European immigrants, many who were poor and illiterate. After they learned the realities of garrison life, the five-year enlistment period seemed endless to many. Fort Laramie suffered from the frontier army desertion rate of 33 percent between 1865 and 1890. (Courtesy of the FLNHS.)

This old guardhouse was erected in 1866. Discipline was harsh in the army life of Fort Laramie. Minor infractions often drew severe penalties, including confinement in the bare, unheated guardhouse. Deserters were usually captured and brought back to the fort to serve time in the guardhouse and perform hard labor while attached to a ball and chain. (Courtesy of the FLNHS.)

Spotted Tail, headman among the Brule Sioux, had participated in the Grattan Massacre in 1854 and had been party to attacks on mail wagons. Gen. William Harney demanded his surrender, and Spotted Tail surrendered at Fort Laramie in October 1855. He was taken to Fort Leavenworth and remained there for several months. He was released in September 1856 to return to his people. Spotted Tail developed a conciliatory attitude toward the white immigrants and was influential in establishing peaceful relations between the whites and Native Americans. (Courtesy of Wyoming State Archives, Department of State Parks and Cultural Resources.)

In March 1866, Spotted Tail brought the body of his daughter, Mini-Aku, for burial among the whites at Fort Laramie, as he had promised her he would. In the summer of 1864, she had been a familiar figure at Fort Laramie. It was reported that she spent long hours on a bench by Sutler's Store, where she was fond of watching the guard mount and the dress parade. She refused to marry one of her own people, attempted to learn English, and advocated for peace with the whites. When the Sioux went on the warpath in 1864, however, Spotted Tail and Mini-Aku were with them and spent the next year in the Powder River country. Mini-Aku became sick and died during the cold winter of 1865–1866. She was buried in the typical Sioux fashion at this purported burial site at Fort Laramie. However, this photograph, taken in 1881, probably shows a replica of the original burial scaffold. By then, her father had already removed her remains and taken them to his reservation. (Courtesy of Wyoming State Archives, Department of State Parks and Cultural Resources.)

Red Cloud, an Oglala Sioux chief, was the only Plains Indian leader to deal the U.S. Army a strategic defeat during the Native American wars. Red Cloud refused to sign the 1868 treaty until the army withdrew from the Bozeman Trail, and he was successful in compelling government forces to surrender both territory and forts. Red Cloud twice visited Washington, D.C., to meet with government leaders, and he gave a speech in New York City in 1870. He fought to have his people remain in the Fort Laramie area, but he eventually lost that battle. Red Cloud and his followers were moved to a reservation on the White River by 1873. (Courtesy of FLNHS.)

Young Man Afraid of his Horses posed for this photograph around 1878. A decade earlier, the Indian brave attended the treaty negotiations with the peace commissioners in Fort Laramie but was not one of the treaty signers. His father, Old Man Afraid of His Horses, was one of the Native Americans who signed the 1868 treaty. (Courtesy of Wyoming State Archives, Department of State Parks and Cultural Resources.)

John "Portugee" Phillips (seated) and Maj. James W. Powell were both involved in Native American conflicts. Phillips, a trader and scout, made a legendary ride from Fort Phil Kearney to Fort Laramie in December 1866 to deliver messages to the commanding officer. Capt. William Fetterman and 80 men had been annihilated by Native Americans led by Crazy Horse and Red Cloud. The fort and its remaining garrison were in danger of being overwhelmed, and the nearest aid lay at Fort Laramie, 236 miles away. Much has been written of Phillips's ride to Fort Laramie, most of it myth. The cold and snowy ride took four days, culminating in Phillips's arrival at Fort Laramie on Christmas night. It was said that Phillips's horse died upon arrival, but that story has no supporting documentation. Major Powell was in command in August 1867 when the Sioux under Crazy Horse attacked his soldiers while gathering wood. Powell's troops were successful in fighting off the natives in a skirmish dubbed the Wagon Box Fight. (Courtesy of FLNHS.)

Fort Laramie had grown to a sizable complex by the time this photograph was taken in 1884. Like most western forts, Fort Laramie had no surrounding stockade because of its size and because Native Americans posed little threat to the post. Soldiers from Fort Laramie fought a number of engagements with natives, but the fort itself was attacked only once during its history. In the summer of 1864, twenty years before this photograph was taken, a small cavalry patrol had just returned to the fort and unsaddled their horses to let them roll on the parade grounds. Suddenly a daring party of 30 Native American warriors dashed through the fort, drove the horses off to the north, and escaped with all but the poorest animals. The soldiers gave chase, but the Native Americans eluded them, as it was difficult to locate and engage hostile natives in the vast expanses of the plains. (Courtesy of FLNHS.)

The peace commissioners are shown in 1868. From left to right are Gen. A. H. Terry, Gen. W. S. Harney, Gen. W. H. Sherman, unidentified Sioux, N. G. Taylor, S. F. Tappan, and C. C. Augur. An earlier conference, in 1851, set for Fort Laramie, was moved 30 miles east on Horse Creek to accommodate thousands of Native Americans and their horses. The resulting treaty provided the immigrants safe travel, while the natives were to receive $50,000 in goods each year. (Courtesy of Wyoming State Archives, Department of State Parks and Cultural Resources.)

The 1851 peace treaty was soon broken by both sides. The Native Americans became alarmed at the steady influx of immigrants, and they were opposed to new forts in the north along the Bozeman Trail. Sioux leaders agreed to gather with the peace commission at Fort Laramie in 1868. Included in this group are post sutler William G. Bullock (center, gray-bearded) and local Indian trader James Bordeaux (standing, far right). The others are unidentified. (Courtesy of Wyoming State Archives, Department of State Parks and Cultural Resources.)

In April and May 1868, the peace commissioners met with various tribes at Fort Laramie. This photograph shows the commissioners with representatives of the Cheyenne and Arapaho tribes. Twenty-five chiefs, including Spotted Tail, Red Leaf, and Swift Bear, were the first to sign a treaty on April 29. By late May, other Native Americans had signed the treaty, but Red Cloud did not attend and refused to sign until the troops had left the Powder River country. Red Cloud continued to maintain a siege on the Bozeman Trail until three forts were vacated in August. Red Cloud finally came to Fort Laramie and signed the treaty on November 6, 1868. The Native Americans were awarded all of what is now South Dakota, west of the Missouri River, and the control and hunting rights of the territory north of the North Platte River and east of the Bighorn Mountains. However, the main object of the treaty was to move free-roaming tribes toward European-style civilization. The Indian agencies were to be located on the Missouri River, but many of the natives objected to giving up trading at Fort Laramie. (Courtesy of Wyoming State Archives, Department of State Parks and Cultural Resources.)

These unidentified soldiers and Native Americans are shown at Fort Laramie during the 1868 treaty negotiations. Despite the newly signed treaty, the Indian wars continued. Whites ignored the treaty by traveling to Montana and the Black Hills in search of gold. The natives scored a short-lived victory by defeating Bvt. Maj. Gen. George Custer in the Battle of Little Bighorn on June 25, 1876. However, by the late 1870s, most Native Americans were confined to reservations. (Courtesy of Wyoming State Archives, Department of State Parks and Cultural Resources.)

A group of unidentified civilians, soldiers, and Native Americans are shown at Fort Laramie during the 1868 treaty negotiations. (Courtesy of the Wyoming State Archives, Department of State Parks and Cultural Resources.)

Native Americans continued to camp near Fort Laramie, as shown in this photograph, taken during the 1868 treaty negotiations. Red Cloud protested being moved from Fort Laramie, and his followers expected to receive their government allotments at Fort Laramie, as they had for years. Finally, in 1873, after Red Cloud and other chiefs had twice traveled to Washington, D.C., and New York, Red Cloud agreed to have his agency moved north to a site on the White River. (Courtesy of the Wyoming State Archives, Department of State Parks and Cultural Resources.)

Most of Fort Laramie's soldiers belonged to infantry units, such as this company of the 7th Infantry. During the 1860s and 1870s, when the army conducted extended campaigns, foot soldiers were most in evidence. They marched five or six hours a day in long columns, four abreast if possible, often accompanied by cavalry and artillery. (Courtesy of the Wyoming State Archives, Department of State Parks and Cultural Resources.)

James A. King served as president of the King Bridge and Manufacturing Company of Cleveland, Ohio. King and his company received the contract and constructed the iron bridge over the Laramie River at Fort Laramie in 1875. (Courtesy of FLNHS.)

This is King's iron bridge over the Laramie River, constructed in 1875 at a cost of $10,500. The bridge served as a vital link on the road between Cheyenne and the Black Hills. It provided an all-season crossing of the river for stagecoaches, miners, and troops passing through Fort Laramie. The bridge remained in use until the 1960s and stands today as a landmark, though its use is confined to foot traffic. (Courtesy of FLNHS.)

Gen. Luther P. Bradley commanded the 9th Infantry, and he served as the commander at Fort Laramie from 1874 to 1875. (Courtesy of FLNHS.)

Lt. Col. Andrew Burt, 7th Infantry, served two different terms at Fort Laramie. In November 1876, Burt, then a captain, led an expedition, headed by Prof. Othniel Marsh of Yale University, to study fossils in the Black Hills. Red Cloud denied them permission to enter the Sioux territory, but the troops made camp, and Captain Burt led the expedition on its way during the night. The Sioux quickly caught up with them and kept them under surveillance but did not attack. Marsh showed his gratitude by meeting with Red Cloud and documenting Sioux grievances, which he conveyed to friends in Washington, D.C. (Courtesy of FLNHS.)

Elizabeth Reynolds Burt, wife of Lt. Col. Andrew Burt, lived at Fort Laramie and raised a family there. (Courtesy of FLNHS.)

Edith Burt was nine years old when this photograph was taken. She lived at Fort Laramie with her parents, Lt. Col. Andrew and Elizabeth Burt. (Courtesy of FLNHS.)

Reynolds J. Burt, the youngest son of Lt. Col. Andrew and Elizabeth Burt, is shown in this photograph. Reynolds lived at Fort Laramie from 1887 to 1888, during his father's second term of duty at the fort. Reynolds wrote that baseball, footracing, horse racing, cards, reading, and talking were all diversions used by soldiers to combat the loneliness and monotony of life at the fort. (Courtesy of FLNHS.)

This house at Fort Laramie was the home of Lt. Col. Andrew and Elizabeth Burt and their family during Burt's second term of duty at the fort. The house came to be known as the Burt House and is one of the buildings remaining at the fort today. Reynolds Burt, who lived in the house as a child, visited the fort in later life, and he described the furnishings and their placement when he had lived there. (Courtesy of FLNHS.)

Lt. Thaddeus H. Capron served at Fort Laramie with C Company, 9th Infantry. He had been out on patrol with troops that had marched from Fort Laramie in late May 1876 under the command of Gen. George Crook. His detachment had not joined in the Battle of Little Bighorn on June 25–26. News of Bvt. Maj. Gen. George Armstrong Custer's defeat at the Little Bighorn was received at Fort Laramie on July 5, 1876, causing much excitement at the fort. The Native Americans had achieved a great victory, decimating five companies of the 7th Cavalry and killing Custer. (Courtesy of FLNHS.)

Cynthia Capron, wife of Lt. Thaddeus Capron, expressed her fear that "the Indians could very easily take the post." Though the fort was not attacked, there continued to be skirmishes throughout the area that kept the troops on constant alert. The Sioux had won the battle, but in the end, they lost the war and were eventually confined to reservations. By the end of 1876, Fort Laramie hosted a large garrison, including six companies of cavalry and five of infantry. The winter was fairly quiet, and by spring of 1877, the Great Sioux War had finally ended. (Courtesy of FLNHS.)

Henry Capron was the son of Lt. Thaddeus and Cynthia Capron. The two-year-old child died at Fort Laramie on June 6, 1876, of tubercular meningitis and was buried in the post cemetery on June 8. His father was in the field and received word of his son's death on June 22. He traveled back to Fort Laramie near the end of June for a brief visit before returning to the field. Lieutenant Capron was later stationed at Fort D. A. Russell, and Henry's body was moved to the fort cemetery near Cheyenne. (Courtesy of FLNHS.)

The Rustic Hotel, located on the west side of Fort Laramie, is shown in this photograph from around 1883. Post trader John S. Collins built the Rustic Hotel in 1876 halfway between Cheyenne and the Black Hills to serve travelers. The Rustic served as a stage station for the Cheyenne–to–Black Hills stage, and the complex included stables and corrals for horses. (Courtesy of FLNHS.)

The manager and guests of the Rustic Hotel are shown in this photograph, taken around 1883. From left to right are unidentified, James Hogle (manager of the Rustic Hotel) holding baby Myrtle Hogle, unidentified, Mrs. Hogle, two unidentified, B. A. Hart (on the step), and Old Harvey (the cook). (Courtesy of FLNHS.)

A group of people are shown by the cellar at the back of the Rustic Hotel. From left to right are unidentified, James Hogle, Old Harvey (the Rustic Hotel cook), and two unidentified. (Courtesy of FLNHS.)

The Cheyenne–to–Black Hills stagecoach traveled toward Fort Laramie from Chugwater in this photograph from the 1880s. In a strange turn of events, outlaws had replaced Native Americans as the major source of trouble. Many of the coaches were robbed, so Fort Laramie provided guards to ride aboard the stages between the post and the Black Hills. (Courtesy of the Wyoming State Archives, Department of State Parks and Cultural Resources.)

Soldiers are shown on the south lawn of the Fort Laramie hospital in the summer of 1888. They are, from left to right, Capt. Louis Brechemin (assistant surgeon), John Tomamichael (hospital steward), a Private Schmidt, a Private Wheeler, a Private Hutcheson, a Private Thorn, a Private Geiger, and a Private Dogotchin. (Courtesy of FLNHS.)

This is a view of the hospital from the northeast around the 1880s. The hospital was built on the site of the old cemetery. According to accounts of the day, the hospital's 12 beds were enough for most situations but were inadequate when an epidemic hit the post. (Courtesy of the National Library of Medicine, from the FLNHS collection.)

Elizabeth Tomamichael, the wife of hospital steward John Tomamichael, is shown in this photograph from 1888. (Courtesy of FLNHS.)

The fort hospital contained a dispensary, a kitchen, a dining room, isolation rooms, and a surgeon's office but no laboratories or operating rooms. Most patients were treated in the surgeon's home office, then, if necessary, were confined to the hospital to recuperate. (Courtesy of the National Library of Medicine, from the FLNHS collection.)

These homes on officers' row are shown in the mid-1880s. Houses flanked by trees and surrounded by picket fences show that nearing the end of the military era at Fort Laramie, the quarters had become quite livable by the standards of the day. Shown from left are Old Bedlam, a pair of company officers' quarters, the surgeon's house, and the Burt House. (Courtesy of FLNHS.)

Officers' row had gained many major improvements in the 1880s. This 1887 view of the officers' homes showed the addition of trees, grass, gaslights, a boardwalk, picket fences, vine-covered verandas, and even a birdbath. The house with the three dormer windows was the commanding officer's quarters. (Courtesy of FLNHS.)

This photograph shows soldiers drilling on the parade ground in front of the officers' quarters buildings B, C, and D, around 1883. Prior to 1870, privates had received $16 per month in pay; after 1870, Congress cut the monthly pay to $13. Weather, bad roads, hostiles, and bandits often delayed the paymaster from arriving at the fort, so that four to six months between paydays was not uncommon. (Courtesy of FLNHS.)

This 1880s view of Fort Laramie shows, from left to right, the old hospital, the sutler's residence, the new hospital, the cavalry barracks, and an unidentified building at the far right. (Courtesy of FLNHS.)

A new administration building was constructed in 1885. The post headquarters were moved to this concrete building. It also served as the post adjutant's office and library. The building also contained a theater, where plays were often performed by the officers and their families during the late 1880s. The theater also served as a chapel. (Courtesy of FLNHS, from the Signal Corps collection.)

A guard mount is shown drilling in front of the administration building around 1889. Soldiers were required to take their turn at the unpopular rotating tours of guard duty. Guard duty ran 24 hours a day in fair and foul weather. Men were also assigned to construction and repair work, including ice-cutting in the winter, warehouse duties, water hauling, and numerous other tasks. (Courtesy of FLNHS, from the Signal Corps collection.)

Soldiers are shown marching around 1884. Pvt. Hervey Johnson, stationed at Fort Laramie from 1863 to 1866, described a day's routine for the cavalry. "The bugle sounded at daylight . . . 20 minutes later every man must be ready . . . roll was called . . . the men marched to the stables to care for the horses . . . then breakfast . . . then the guards were mounted and placed at their posts . . . followed by noon dinner . . . afternoon drill call . . . evening care of the horses . . . supper . . . and lights out by 9:15 p.m." (Courtesy of FLNHS.)

The troops were camped near Fort Laramie in this photograph, taken around 1885. (Courtesy of FLNHS.)

Thomas Sandercock served as the post engineer at Fort Laramie from 1883 to 1887. He died on December 20, 1887. (Courtesy of FLNHS.)

Harriet "Hattie" Sandercock was the wife of Thomas Sandercock. She lived at Fort Laramie during her husband's tour of duty and for many years thereafter. (Courtesy of FLNHS.)

Capt. Thomas Bull DeWees, 2nd Cavalry, was stationed at Fort Laramie in 1867 and 1868. He served as the commanding officer of Company A, 2nd Cavalry. (Courtesy of FLNHS.)

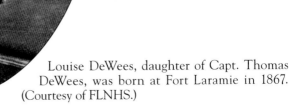

Louise DeWees, daughter of Capt. Thomas DeWees, was born at Fort Laramie in 1867. (Courtesy of FLNHS.)

Several "hog ranches" were established outside the military reservation, where the soldiers obtained liquor and prostitutes. Adolph Cuny and Julius Ecoffey ran the Three Mile Ranch, located 3 miles from Fort Laramie. Soldiers sometimes suffered dire consequences after visiting these ranches. Punishment for infractions often resulted in confinement at the post guardhouse, including hard labor. Some soldiers died, due to alcoholic poisoning or fighting. (Courtesy of the FLNHS.)

This photograph, taken at the Three Mile Ranch, shows a building at the hog ranch, which was located 3 miles west of Fort Laramie. The complex included a warehouse, a bunkhouse, an ice house, a blacksmith shop, a billiard hall and saloon, a sod corral, and 6 two-room cottages, one for each "working girl." (Courtesy of the FLNHS.)

Adolph Cuny was a U.S. marshal and part owner of the Three Mile Ranch. Cuny was murdered at the Six Mile Hog Ranch, which he also operated, in July 1877. Cuny was shot after he had gone to the Six Mile to assist in the arrest of members of an outlaw gang. (Courtesy of FLNHS.)

A group of unidentified officers and civilians are shown on the front porch of officers' quarters B in the summer of 1885. (Courtesy of FLNHS.)

This building, officers' quarters A, was constructed in 1870. It was planned as the commanding officer's quarters, but it was divided into a duplex for company grade officers. When a new officer was assigned to the post, he could "rank out of quarters" any junior officer and take the house for his own. The house is shown as it appears today. (Courtesy of the author.)

This photograph shows a group of unidentified officers at Fort Laramie in 1885. The garrison during the military's waning years consisted of from four to six companies of the 7th Infantry. The railroad had bypassed the fort a few years earlier, and the fort's usefulness had declined by the end of the 1880s. (Courtesy of FLNHS.)

Guards are shown protecting the vegetable garden at Fort Laramie around 1883. The post garden yielded varied produce, including corn, potatoes, and onions. (Courtesy of FLNHS.)

Sgt. Leodegar Schnyder left Fort Laramie on October 13, 1886, after serving with distinction for 37 years at the same location. Sergeant Schnyder had arrived at Fort Laramie as a member of the 6th Infantry in 1849. Sergeant Schnyder had wisely declined an invitation to accompany Bvt. 2nd Lt. John Grattan on the fateful journey to the Sioux camp in 1854 after he had issued munitions to Grattan from his position as ordnance sergeant. (Courtesy of FLNHS.)

Julia Gill was a laundress at Fort Laramie before she met and married Sgt. Leodegar Schnyder. She was the second wife of Sergeant Schnyder and continued to reside at Fort Laramie with her husband. Upon his retirement, a news article noted that the 7th Infantry band serenaded the sergeant and his wife, "cross-eyed Julia," as they left Fort Laramie. (Courtesy of FLNHS.)

Sergeant Schnyder served as postmaster at Fort Laramie from 1859 to 1876. 1st Lt. James Regan wrote this description. "From the post trader's it is but a few steps to the post office, which is in one of the primitive adobe buildings. The interior is divided into two rooms, one of which was used as the postal-room, and the other as the abode of Postmaster and Ordnance Sergeant Leodegar Schnyder, who marched here with the first troops in '49 and has been in this one isolated post ever since." The post office is shown as it looks today, with the exterior restored to its 1880s appearance. (Courtesy of the author.)

Charlotte and Charles Schnyder were two of the children of Sgt. Leodegar Schnyder and his wife, Julia. (Courtesy of FLNHS.)

Officers and children are shown in front of buildings on officers' row in 1889. Some records show the identities are, from left to right, Lt. Levi F. Burnett, a little boy named Howell, Isabelle Howell, Kitty Johnson, Sallie Kirtland, Doris Frederick, Ada Howell, and Lt. Alfred Johnson. The children are from the families of officers stationed at the fort. (Courtesy of FLNHS.)

A group of young people known as the "Kindergarten" posed on the lawn of the commanding officers' quarters in the summer of 1889. Shown in the first row (on the lawn) are, from left to right, Lt. Frederic Sargeant, 7th Infantry; Kitty Boyd; and Steve Mizner, a visitor from the 4P Ranch; (second row) Helen Worden, Lillian Brechemin, and Carrie Merriam; (third row) Lt. George W. McIver, 7th Infantry. (Courtesy of FLNHS.)

This ornate, Victorian-style home served as the sutler's residence around 1878. G. H. Collins, the sutler at that time, is standing by the gate. Mrs. G. H. Collins is seated on the porch, and their daughter, Nettie Collins, is standing near the door. This house was remodeled over the years but is no longer standing. (Courtesy of FLNHS.)

A group poses in the yard of the sutler's house in 1886. Shown from left to right are (seated on the ground) John London Jr. and Stephen Mizner from the 4P ranch; (seated in the second row) John London, the post trader (or sutler); Lucy London; Mrs. Louis Brechemin; and Lonnie Hall; (standing) Capt. Louis Brechemin, Josephine Sprague, Eli Hall, and Maude Hall. (Courtesy of FLNHS.)

Col. Henry C. Merriam is shown in his military uniform in this undated photograph. Colonel Merriam was post commander at Fort Laramie from 1884 to 1889. Though Fort Laramie was fairly calm during Colonel Merriam's tenure, he believed that the troops still needed to practice marching. In the fall of 1886, he instructed each of his companies to conduct a 10-day march to Laramie Peak and back with full field equipment. (Courtesy of FLNHS.)

Col. Henry C. Merriam, along with his family and friends, is shown in this 1888 photograph. Pictured on the lawn of the commanding officer's house are, from left to right, Henry's wife, Una Merriam; baby Maude Merriam; Henry M. Merriam; Col. Henry C. Merriam; Charles Merriam; Carrie Merriam; Kitty Boyd; and Cyrus Merriam. (Courtesy of FLNHS.)

This is a photograph of the wife of Col. Henry C. Merriam. She resided at Fort Laramie, where she raised a family and hosted various events at the fort. During the Merriams' residence at Fort Laramie, there was little military action occurring. The Merriams and other military families participated in many social events at the fort. (Courtesy of FLNHS.)

This photograph shows participants in a performance presented at the fort in 1889. They are, from left to right, (first row) Helen Worden, playing Helen of Troy; Carrie Merriam, playing Jeptha's daughter; and Lillian Brechemin, playing Joan of Arc; (second row) Mrs. Louis Brechemin, playing Queen Eleanor; Col. Henry Merriam, playing King Edward III; and Julia Howell, as the reader; (third row) Kitty Boyd, playing Cleopatra, and Steve Mizner, playing Dick Swiveler. (Courtesy of FLNHS.)

A group of unidentified officers and ladies pose on the porch of Col. Henry C. Merriam's residence around 1884. (Courtesy of FLNHS.)

These officers' daughters were dressed in fancy costumes for an unknown occasion in the summer of 1886. Shown from left to right are Lillian Brechemin, Carrie Merriam, Fanny Comba, and Helen Worden. (Courtesy of FLNHS.)

This photograph shows some of the officers' daughters in the summer of 1888, driving a horse and cart. Shown from left to right are Carrie Merriam, Helen Worden, and Lillian Brechemin. (Courtesy of FLNHS.)

In the summer of 1888, riders are shown fording the Laramie River near the footbridge below the quartermaster's office. They are, from left to right, (on horseback) Kathie Booth (on Jim), Fannie Comba (on Billie), Reynolds Burt (on Buck), Lillian Brechemin (on Dick), Kitty Johnson and Ada Howell (on Sorrel), and Lucie London and Toots Merriam (on Chubbie). The women standing on the bank at right are Mrs. Louis Brechemin (left) and Mrs. C. A. Booth (holding the umbrella). (Courtesy of FLNHS.)

Capt. Louis Brechemin was the post surgeon, occupying a prestigious position at Fort Laramie. Shown in front of the Brechemin house in 1888 are, from left to right, Capt. Louis Brechemin, Lonnie Hall, Martha Frederick, Kitty Boyd, Mrs. Bowness Briggs, Helen Worden, Carrie Merriam, Edward Frederick, Kitty Johnson, Capt. Constant Williams, Lucy London, Edith Burt, Mrs. Louis Brechemin, lst Lt. Van Orsdale, Elizabeth Burt, lst Lt. D. A. Frederick, Mrs. Charles Booth, Julia Howell, and Lt. Col. Andrew Burt. Seated on the boardwalk are Jim Howell and Ada Howell. (Courtesy of FLNHS.)

The Brechemin family and guests are shown on the veranda of their home in 1888. Pictured from left to right are (seated on the floor) Lillian Brechemin; (second row) Bowness Briggs of the Wilmington Northern Railroad, Capt. Louis Brechemin, and Mrs. Bowness Briggs; (third row) Mrs. Louis Brechemin and Louis Brechemin Jr. (Courtesy of FLNHS.)

Officers and families posed in this 1888 photograph. Shown from left to right are (first row) Toots Merriam, Bessie Comba, Rachel Johnson, Kitty Johnson, Charlotte Benham, Henry Merriam Jr., and lst Lt. John L. Barber; (second row) Delia Comba, Mrs. Richard Comba, Mrs. Bowness Briggs, Mrs. Albert Johnson, Martha Frederick, Edward Frederick, Mrs. Louis Brechemin, Kathie Booth, and Capt. Richard Comba; (third row) Fannie Comba, Carrie Merriam, Mrs. D. W. Benham, and Una Merriam; (fourth row) Louis Brechemin Jr., Lillian Brechemin, lst Lt. D. A. Frederick, Col. Henry C. Merriam, baby Charles Merriam, Lonnie Hall, Kitty Boyd, Edith Burt, and Bowness Briggs; (fifth row) lst Lt. Van Orsdale, Charles Merriam, Capt. Robert B. Benham, Capt. Louis Brechemin, Maj. D. W. Benham, and lst Lt. Charles A. Worden. (Courtesy of FLNHS.)

A group of people are pictured on a summer outing near Fort Laramie in the late 1880s. From left to right are (first row) Johnnie Gibbon and John London; (second row) Lonnie Hall; (third row) Genevieve Sanno, Eli Hall, Neely Williams, and 2nd Lt. Tommy Tompkins. (Courtesy of FLNHS.)

Neely Williams lived at Fort Laramie with her family in the late 1880s. She was the daughter of Capt. Constant Williams, 7th Infantry. (Courtesy of FLNHS.)

Friends from Fort Laramie are shown having a picnic on a creek near Hartville, north of Fort Laramie, in the summer of 1889. They are, from left to right, 1st Lt. L. D. Greene, Mary Buckley, Louis Brechemin Jr., and Mrs. Louis Brechemin Sr. (Courtesy of FLNHS.)

Some of the officers' children are shown riding near Deer Creek in 1886. They are, from left to right, Louis Brechemin Jr. (holding a horse), Lillian Brechemin (on Dick), Fannie Comba (on Billie), Sollace Coolidge (holding a horse), and Helen Worden (on Chubbie.) (Courtesy of FLNHS.)

71

The officers' quarters building, dubbed "Old Bedlam," gained quite a reputation during its early days at Fort Laramie, when it housed bachelor officers. However, toward the end of the military era at Fort Laramie, many officers and their wives and families lived in the complex. It is believed that this photograph shows the wife and children of Lt. Daniel L. Howell on the porch of Old Bedlam in 1889. (Courtesy of FLNHS.)

Old Bedlam is pictured near the end of the military era at Fort Laramie in 1889. By that time, there were large trees lining the parade ground to the west of Old Bedlam. The parade ground was covered with grass, in contrast to its dirt and gravel appearance when the fort was first occupied by the military in 1849. (Courtesy of FLNHS.)

Troops from Fort Laramie participated in drills at nearby forts, as shown in this photograph of the soldiers at Fort Robinson in 1889. The long-anticipated directive to abandon Fort Laramie finally came down in the late summer of 1889, while most of the garrison was absent, attending a camp at Fort Robinson. Most of the troops marched out of the fort that fall. A skeleton crew, under the direction of Lt. George W. McIver, remained at the fort from the fall of 1889 to the spring of 1890. Lieutenant McIver wrote, "The winter seemed long and monotonous. Fortunately, the daylight hours were pretty well taken up with the work of packing, invoicing and shipping away the property and equipment. In the spring of 1890, Lt. Charles W. Taylor, Quartermaster of the 9th Cavalry, made two trips to Fort Laramie with a large wagon train, each time hauling away a large amount of material and equipment for use at Fort Robinson." (Courtesy of FLNHS.)

John Hunton arrived at Fort Laramie as a young man in 1867. He hired on as a bullwhacker on a freight train carrying goods from Nebraska City to Fort Laramie. Shortly after his arrival at the fort, he secured a job clerking in Sutler's Store, where he worked for four years. Hunton subsequently secured several contracts with the army during the 1870s to supply wood, hay, and beef to Forts Laramie and Fetterman. He also established a cattle ranch 25 miles southwest of the fort. Hunton became the last post trader at Fort Laramie in 1888. (Courtesy of FLNHS.)

John Hunton is shown riding his favorite "Sam Hoss," crossing the Laramie River near Fort Laramie. (Courtesy of FLNHS.)

Three

THE HOMESTEADERS

This is a view of Fort Laramie in 1889, shortly before the army abandoned the post and auctioned off most of the buildings at the post. Thus began the era of the homesteaders at Fort Laramie. However, before the buildings were sold, a detachment of the 9th Cavalry from Fort Robinson, returned to salvage anything that might be useful there. They removed doors, windows, and flooring from many of the buildings. (Courtesy of FLNHS.)

This 1898 view shows Fort Laramie during the homestead era. Nineteen people paid a total of $1,417 for 35 buildings at the April 9, 1890, auction. The army sold only the structures, not the land on which they stood, since the entire military reservation, nearly 3,400 acres, was transferred to the Department of the Interior for eventual return to the public domain. Many of the buildings were removed or their parts salvaged. Some buyers squatted on the land until they were able to acquire the land as homesteads. (Courtesy of FLNHS.)

Old Bedlam, pictured in 1898, was one of the 18 buildings purchased by John Hunton during the 1890 auction. Hunton occasionally rented out Old Bedlam for school classes, like the one shown in this photograph. Pictured from left to right are (seated in the first row) Meade Sandercock, Rosie Neidfelt, and Mary Neidfelt; (seated in the second row) Leo Wolf; (third row) Frank Hopkins, Laura Neidfelt, Martha Neidfelt, unidentified, and Louis Wilde. (Courtesy of FLNHS.)

These buildings, all owned by John Hunton, included Old Bedlam (left), officers' quarters E and F, the surgeon's house, and the Burt House. They are shown in 1899. Hunton was appointed the last post trader in 1888, but he was left holding a store full of goods on a vacant army post when the fort closed. That left him heavily in debt, and he spent several years selling or renting many of the buildings he had purchased. (Courtesy of FLNHS.)

Perhaps the handsomest and most significant building at the fort, Old Bedlam, was saved in large part because of the efforts of John Hunton. Seen here in 1902, Old Bedlam was still in good condition. (Courtesy of FLNHS.)

Joe and Mary Wilde purchased the cavalry barracks at the 1890 government auction. The Wildes purchased the stock of goods from John Hunton and established a store on the ground floor of the barracks. During the army days, the Wildes had lived 9 miles west of Fort Laramie. Joe worked as a government teamster, and Mary sold butter and eggs to the garrison through the Trader's Store. (Courtesy of the author.)

The cavalry barracks was the largest building at Fort Laramie. The owners, Joe and Mary Wilde, transformed the cavernous two-story barracks into a store, a saloon, a dance hall, a shoe shop, and a 12-room hotel. Their venture became a popular social center for farmers and ranchers in the area. They hosted the first of many raucous all-night dances on July 4, 1892. (Courtesy of FLNHS.)

Joe Wilde is shown here in 1915. He was a former freighter and quartermaster employee at Fort Laramie. He purchased the cavalry barracks for $50 at the government auction. Wilde later acquired the commissary building, shown in the background, from John Hunton. (Courtesy of FLNHS.)

Joe Wilde also started a feed and coal store in the commissary building, which was also used to house animals. However, the Wildes sold their interests at Fort Laramie in 1917. (Courtesy of FLNHS.)

The cavalry barracks continued to be a center for gatherings in the Fort Laramie area. In this photograph, a banner on the cavalry barracks announces the upcoming rodeo and dance, set for August 22, 1924, sponsored by the American Legion Post 69. (Courtesy of FLNHS.)

Joe Wilde sold the cavalry barracks to Louis Carlson, who then sold it to a man named Clarke. A portion of the building became a summer retreat under Clarke. He remodeled the south end of the building into quarters for sharecrop tenants and hired Harry and Tom Latta, from Mitchell, Nebraska, to manage the operation. (Courtesy of FLNHS.)

Bill Latta is shown tending his beet field at Fort Laramie around 1920 in the above photograph. The field was located near the commissary building. The photograph below shows a view of Fort Laramie during the homesteaders era, around 1915. (Both, courtesy of FLNHS.)

John and Blanche Hunton pose in front of the Burt House. They lived in this house at Fort Laramie for several years after Hunton purchased the house. This had been the home of Lt. Col. Andrew Burt and his family during his second tenure at Fort Laramie. Hunton also became the commissioner for the General Land Office and operated a blacksmith shop at Fort Laramie. (Courtesy of Wyoming State Archives, Department of Parks and Cultural Resources.)

This photograph shows the side and rear of the Burt House. The person at the side door is unidentified. (Courtesy of FLNHS.)

The surgeon's house (left), the Burt House (center), and Sutler's Store are shown in the above photograph in the 1930s. John Hunton owned all of these buildings. Hunton rented out both the surgeon's house and the Burt House at various times. Shown below, from left to right, are Old Bedlam, the surgeon's house, the Burt House, and Sutler's Store in this 1920s photograph. (Both, courtesy of FLNHS.)

The Flannery family poses in front of the Burt House in the 1920s. L. G. "Pat" Flannery moved with his wife, Alice, and their daughter, Billie, to Fort Laramie in 1921. He was a close friend of John Hunton and the benefactor of Hunton's diaries after Hunton's death. After Flannery retired, he spent the last years of his life organizing and editing the Hunton diaries for publication. (Courtesy of FLNHS.)

This photograph shows furniture belonging to the Flannerys when they rented the Burt House from John Hunton. These were the furnishings in the 1920s in the parlor of the Burt House. Pat Flannery founded a weekly newspaper, the *Fort Laramie Scout*, in 1923, which he later combined with the *Goshen County News*. Flannery was later instrumental in securing Fort Laramie as a part of the U.S. National Park System. (Courtesy of FLNHS.)

The above photograph shows a view of the buildings at Fort Laramie in the 1930s. Sutler's Store is seen on the left, the cavalry barracks on the right, and the hospital ruins on the hill in the background of the photograph. The photograph below shows the bakery in the right foreground, the commissary to the back of the bakery, and a glimpse of the cavalry barracks behind the trees. (Both, courtesy of FLNHS.)

Both of these photographs show the old guardhouse in the 1920s and 1930s. John Hunton originally purchased the old guardhouse at the army auction. He sold it to George Corey, who used the building as a residence for a short time. Hattie Sandercock owned the old guardhouse at some point, and she used it as storage, a barn, and a chicken coop. (Both, courtesy of FLNHS.)

John and Blanche Hunton are shown in front of the non-commissioned officers' quarters around 1910. Hunton also purchased this large building at the 1890 auction and began tearing it apart for the components. He later sold the building, but it appears the new owners never finished dismantling the building, leaving the southern section intact at the time this photograph was taken. The building was later stripped, but the walls still stand on the hill near the hospital ruins. (Courtesy of FLNHS.)

The surgeon's house was another of John Hunton's purchases that remained in relatively good condition throughout the homestead era of Fort Laramie. In the fort's day, the surgeon maintained his scientific collections and kept data on such things as the weather. Most of his patients were treated in his office in the rear of the building and then might have been sent to the hospital to recuperate. (Courtesy of FLNHS.)

Harriet "Hattie" Sandercock, the widow of post engineer Tom Sandercock, purchased officers' quarters A, situated at the south end of the parade ground. When John Hunton closed his store, which also housed the Fort Laramie Post Office, Hattie Sandercock was appointed postmaster. She established the post office in the front room of her residence in the spring of 1891 and retained the position of postmaster for 10 years. (Courtesy of FLNHS.)

Hattie Sandercock and her seven children lived at the old fort for many years. She eventually homesteaded the land on which her house stood, while some of her children homesteaded land across the Laramie River. Hattie is shown here feeding her flock of chickens in 1909. (Courtesy of FLNHS.)

These young boys are posed in the yard of officers' quarters A with tents and rifles around 1899. The boy on the left is unidentified. The boy on the right is Meade Sandercock, one of the children of Tom and Hattie Sandercock, who grew up in the house his mother purchased from the government in 1890. This house remained on its original site and was occupied by members of the Sandercock family until the property was acquired by the State of Wyoming in 1937. (Courtesy of FLNHS.)

Over the years, from 1890 to 1930, most of the principal buildings and all of the minor buildings at Fort Laramie had been destroyed. Few people were concerned with saving the old fort for posterity. John Hunton lacked the money to maintain the row of buildings on the west side of the parade ground, but he did save many of them from outright destruction. A pivotal moment seems to have been on June 17, 1913, when a large concrete marker was installed north of Sutler's Store and engraved with these words: "Fort Laramie, a Military Post on the Oregon Trail, June 16, 1849–March 2, 1890. This Monument is erected by the State of Wyoming and a Few Interested Residents." Renewed statewide interest was sparked to preserve the old fort when crowds assembled on the parade grounds at the Fort Laramie Wagon Train Centennial Celebration on August 15, 1930. (Courtesy of FLNHS.)

Old Bedlam, the surgeon's house, and the Burt House are shown in this aerial view of the covered wagon centennial and pioneers' reunion on August 15, 1930. It was reported that more than 20,000 people attended the affair, marking the observance of the crossing of the Smith-Jackson-Sublette wagon train from St. Louis to the rendezvous area on the Wind River in southwestern Wyoming. Pat Flannery declared, "The Old Fort lived again, when the largest crowd ever assembled in the North Platte Valley gathered to show their interest in the movement, now rapidly gaining headway, to preserve and restore this birthplace of western history as a state or national monument." Seven years later, the State of Wyoming appropriated funds for the purchase and donation to the federal government of 214 acres of land, including the surviving buildings. (Courtesy of FLNHS.)

Old Bedlam seems to have held a special, and perhaps sentimental, place in the heart of John Hunton. This largest of the frame buildings contained more lumber than perhaps any other building on the post. John Hunton had sold or salvaged lumber from many of the other post buildings he owned, but he did not salvage Old Bedlam, nor did he permit the use of the building by anyone, except when he rented out rooms to local schoolteachers, now and then. (Courtesy FLNHS.)

Though Old Bedlam fell into disrepair over the years, the grand old building was eventually rescued by the many people who were interested in the preservation of old Fort Laramie. Old Bedlam is shown here in its restored condition. (Courtesy of the author.)

Four

THE NATIONAL HISTORIC SITE

The State of Wyoming, through the landmarks commission, acquired the 214.41 acres and the surviving buildings at Fort Laramie for $25,594.75 in 1937. The property was conveyed to the U.S. National Park Service in 1938. This photograph shows a view of Fort Laramie as it looked in 1937. (Courtesy of FLNHS.)

Fittingly, a grand celebration was staged on the fort's parade ground on July 5, 1937, celebrating the acquisition of Fort Laramie by the State of Wyoming. A group of unidentified old-timers posed for this photograph at the dedication ceremony. (Courtesy of FLNHS.)

This deadwood stage was donated to Fort Laramie by James H. Cook on July 5, 1937, during the dedication ceremonies. The people in the photograph are unidentified. The stage is no longer in the fort's collection. (Courtesy of FLNHS.)

William Henry Jackson (right) was the featured speaker at the Fort Laramie dedication ceremony on July 5, 1937. Jackson was a renowned early-day photographer of the American West, and he is best known as the first person to photograph the wonders of Yellowstone. Jackson worked with Dr. Ferdinand Hayden for seven years on the U.S. Geological Survey. The survey took him to unique and unexplored places, which he documented with thousands of photographs. Jackson later operated a photography studio in Denver, Colorado. He took up painting at the age of 81 and completed approximately 100 paintings dealing with historic themes. Jackson had photographed Fort Laramie in 1870 and was 94 years old when he spoke at the dedication ceremony. He died on June 30, 1942, at the age of 99. Many of his works are on display at Scotts Bluff National Monument, which houses the world's largest collection of original William Henry Jackson sketches, paintings, and photographs. (Courtesy of FLNHS.)

Pictured are the unidentified members of a survey crew working to take a survey of the buildings and ruins at Fort Laramie in December 1939. After the fort was acquired by the U.S. National Park Service, there remained much work to be done to rehabilitate the old buildings. (Courtesy of FLNHS.)

This photograph shows the ruins of one of the former officers' quarters buildings. The army had removed the doors and windows for use in other forts, but part of the roof still remained in this 1916 photograph. Even the roof is gone today, and all that remains are the lime-grout walls. (Courtesy of FLNHS.)

The above photograph demonstrates how the old bakery had been used to house livestock in this 1920s or 1930s photograph. It was eventually restored to its original condition. In the 1924 photograph below, chickens and turkeys inhabited the building that had been the post magazine (storehouse for military supplies), which has also been restored. (Both, courtesy of the FLNHS.)

Visitors to Fort Laramie on August 22, 1937, were sitting on the steps of the Hunton House (Burt House). From left to right are George Houser, editor of the *Guernsey Gazette*; Daniel Greenburg, publicity chairman for the landmarks commission; John Atkin; Robert Rymill, local businessman; and Robert Ellison, a historic preservationist from Casper, Wyoming. These men had all been influential in promoting the acquisition of Fort Laramie by the U.S. National Park Service. (Courtesy of the FLNHS.)

The west half of Sutler's Store, which contained the officers' and enlisted men's bars, is shown in this 1930s photograph. The building had fallen into disrepair, as it had served as quarters for livestock and as a storage during the homestead era. (Courtesy of FLNHS.)

This is how Old Bedlam looked on September 3, 1937. John Hunton had somehow kept the beloved old building from falling down, though he sold it in 1920, along with all of his remaining interests at Fort Laramie. Old Bedlam continued to survive, awaiting rescue, which finally happened in the late 1930s. (Courtesy of Wyoming State Archives, Department of Parks and Cultural Resources.)

A large crowd was on hand at a ceremony celebrating the repaired porch and roof of Old Bedlam on August 15, 1940. The ribbon-cutting ceremony also marked the date that Fort Laramie was designated as a national landmark. (Courtesy of the Wyoming State Archives, Department of Parks and Cultural Resources.)

The above photograph shows the rear view of the old guardhouse around 1937. The photograph below, taken in 1955, is a view of the restored solitary confinement cells in the old guardhouse. Visitors today find there is very little light in each tiny, crowded cell. (Both, courtesy of FLNHS.)

The old guardhouse at Fort Laramie is shown in this photograph. Those who spent time in the guardhouse found it an unpleasant place. This structure, used until 1876, accommodated about two dozen prisoners in an unheated and unlighted sub-story room. No furniture was provided, and bedding consisted only of the blankets that the prisoners brought with them. After 1876, the army used the building as a gunpowder magazine (storehouse). (Courtesy of the author.)

This photograph shows how officers' quarters A looked on November 3, 1947. The house had been used for many years, with relatively little alteration. (Courtesy of FLNHS.)

Fort Laramie felt the effects of the famous early-1949 blizzard that blanketed parts of Wyoming, South Dakota, and Nebraska. This photograph shows the snow on buildings at Fort Laramie on January 5, 1949. In the entire area of the storm, 17 people perished, along with 55,000 head of cattle and more than 100,000 sheep. (Courtesy of FLNHS.)

The old bakery is shown in the above photograph in 1939, as it was beginning to fall apart. The photograph below shows the old bakery in 1949, with the roof and one end of the building nearly collapsed. John Hunton had owned the bakery, which he called the granary because the army had used it as a granary. Hunton and other occupants used both the old and new bakeries as barns and corrals for livestock. The new bakery burned as the result of a grass fire that swept the fort in April 1925, leaving only the lime-grout walls, much as they appear today. The old bakery has been restored. (Both, courtesy of FLNHS.)

More than 1,000 people gathered at old Fort Laramie on August 15, 1935, to celebrate the 75th anniversary of the Pony Express. Local Boy Scouts participated in a re-ride, carrying the mail along the original route in relay segments of 5 to 10 miles. The *Goshen News* of August 22, 1935 reported, "Promptly at four o'clock, over the hill, down the old trail galloped a Boy Scout Pony Express rider . . . delivering the mail sack carrying messages from various historic places and organizations to President Roosevelt and officials of the Oregon Trail Association." Among the honored guests was William Henry Jackson, a pioneer, photographer, and member of the Oregon Trail Memorial Association, who is pictured standing in front of an official automobile for the ceremony. (Courtesy of FLNHS.)

More than 200 Wyoming horsemen carried the mail across eight Wyoming counties, following closely the original Pony Express route, in observance of Wyoming's official celebration of the Centennial of the Pony Express. Re-rides commemorating the Pony Express took place over a three-day period from July 23 to July 25, 1960. Eastbound riders reached Fort Laramie on July 25 and are shown exchanging the mail sack, called a *mochila*, to the next group of riders to carry onward. A program at Fort Laramie included speeches by Fred A. Seaton, U.S. Secretary of the Interior, and Conrad Wirth, director of the U.S. National Park Service. (Courtesy of the Wyoming State Archives, Department of State Parks and Cultural Resources.)

The ruins of the lime-grout building that had been erected in 1887 are shown in this photograph. It was the last of several such structures that sheltered steam engines used for sawing wood and pumping water. (Courtesy of the author.)

The ruins of the old sawmill are in the foreground of this photograph, and the hospital ruins are in the background on the hill. The principal fuel at Fort Laramie had been wood. It took several dozen cords monthly to supply a post the size of Fort Laramie. Men were sent to the mountains to gather wood and bring it back to the post for sawing into small pieces to stoke the heating and cooking stoves. (Courtesy of the author.)

The covered wagon in the above photograph is similar to those used by the thousands of immigrants who followed the trails headed for the West Coast. The campsite in the photograph below is similar to the way a camp was set up when an immigrant wagon and its occupants stopped at Fort Laramie in the mid-1800s. However, covered wagons during those days would have been quartered outside of the fort, usually at a campground across the Laramie River to the south. The emigrants often stopped at the fort to rest, obtain supplies, and have wagons repaired and animals shod at the fort's blacksmith shop. This camp was set up at a re-enactment of a military camp during a demonstration at Fort Laramie in the summer of 2009. (Both, courtesy of the author.)

Both of these photographs show a re-enactment of a military camp during a demonstration at Fort Laramie in the summer of 2009. The Colorado Unit, Company D, of the 1st Colorado Volunteers, representing the Civil War era of 1862, performed the demonstration. They were re-creating an infantry unit of Company G, the 8th Kansas Volunteers, who were quartered briefly at Fort Laramie in 1861. (Both, courtesy of the author.)

The above photograph shows how the soldiers' tents would have been set up in a typical camp on the Western frontier. The photograph below shows soldiers re-enacting a drill during this military reenactment at Fort Laramie in the summer of 2009. (Both, courtesy of the author.)

Soldiers on drill are shown in the above photograph during a re-enactment ceremony. A re-enactment soldier, dressed in the typical uniform of the 1860s, is shown in the photograph at left. He is talking with a visitor to Fort Laramie during the summer of 2009. (Both, courtesy of the author.)

The entrance to the Fort Laramie National Historic Site is shown in this photograph. The fort looks much as it did when the post was the center of activity in the area, beginning in 1849 as a military post. The historic site is about 3 miles southwest of the town of Fort Laramie, Wyoming, off U.S. Route 26. (Courtesy of the author.)

A stop at the visitor center provides historical information. By following the official map and guide of Fort Laramie, the visitor center is the first location on the map. This building served as the commissary and storehouse around 1884, where the commissary sergeant dispensed foodstuffs to the soldiers. Civilians used the building as a coal dispensary and barn. It now houses park offices and the visitor center. (Courtesy of the author.)

The above photograph shows the restored old bakery, built originally around 1876, and the new bakery ruins, constructed around 1883. Because bread was a staple of the soldier's diet, the bakery was one of the most important buildings at a military post. The photograph below shows the ovens used by the workers. Bakers, working at large, double brick ovens, produced up to 700 eighteen-ounce loaves daily. Companies were allowed a ration of flour, which was usually baked into many 18-ounce loaves of bread. The loaves were then issued to the soldiers as their daily ration of bread. (Both, courtesy of the author.)

Fort Laramie National Historic Site interpreter Brandon Lewis tells visitors how bread was made in the above photograph. Sometimes fresh baked bread samples are available to visitors. The photograph below shows the bakery's storeroom, re-created to look as it would have when the post was in operation. Replicas of loaves of bread are seen on the shelves. (Both, courtesy of the author.)

Laundresses were employed by the army to wash the soldiers clothing. They set up their laundry facilities in a similar location, as shown in this re-enactment photograph, near the Laramie River. The laundresses were paid by the army, and the money was then deducted from a soldier's pay. They usually washed clothing for around 20 soldiers and were paid $1 each per month. Therefore, they received more money than most soldiers did, who were usually paid $13 a month. Some laundresses were the wives of enlisted men or they married enlisted men while employed at the fort. (Courtesy of the author.)

This is a modern-day photograph of the infantry barracks foundation. The former barracks, built around 1867, was a one-story frame building housing three companies. It included mess halls and kitchens for each company at the rear of the building. A typical dinner at the fort might have included bacon, bean soup, bread, and tea, as reported by Pvt. Hervey Johnson in 1865. (Courtesy of the author.)

The new guardhouse was constructed in 1876 in response to frequent complaints from the post surgeon that the guardhouse was unhealthy and overcrowded, with major and minor offenders thrown together. Conditions were better for both guards and prisoners. Prisoners slept on the floor on straw mattresses and blankets. (Courtesy of the author.)

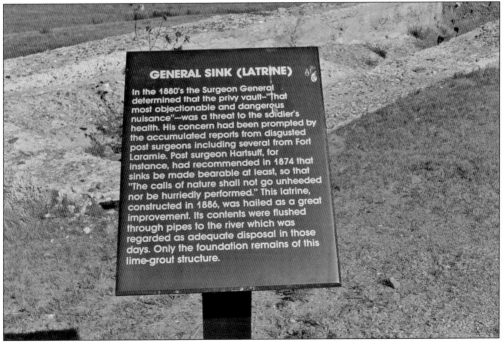

This photograph shows the general sink (latrine) ruins, built in 1886. At the urging of the post surgeon, the facility was built for four companies. The sewerage, however, was channeled from there into the Laramie River. (Courtesy of the author.)

All that remains of the *c.* 1866 infantry barracks for 2 Company is a long, low mound on the southeast side of the parade grounds. (Courtesy of the author.)

The old guardhouse, Fort Laramie's second guardhouse, was built around 1866. It was designed to hold 40 prisoners, doubling the capacity of the first guardhouse, but it often held more. (Courtesy of the author.)

All that is left of the administration building are these concrete ruins. The post headquarters were moved here in 1885. It also served as the post adjutant's office and library. The building also housed a school for the children of enlisted men and some officers. Concerts, religious services, dances, plays, and lectures were presented in the combined theater/chapel in the rear wing. (Courtesy of the author.)

The captain's quarters, built around 1870, was planned as the commanding officers' quarters. However, it was divided into a duplex for company grade officers. It is furnished to its appearance in 1872. The house was home to Hattie Sandercock, the widow of post engineer Thomas Sandercock, and her children from 1890 until 1937, during the homesteaders' era at Fort Laramie. (Courtesy of the author.)

This was the location of the 1858 officers' quarters ruins. Nothing remains of the buildings today. (Courtesy of the author.)

There is no trace of the former adobe structures of Fort John, built by the American Fur Company in 1841. The old fort was located just south of the area that became the parade ground. The army used old Fort John for storage until it was demolished in 1862. (Courtesy of the author.)

These large lime-concrete buildings, two duplexes, and the commanding officers' quarters, were built as major additions to smaller adobe buildings dating from 1855. Doors and windows were removed by the military before the post closed in 1890, and people who purchased the buildings at auction salvaged whatever lumber was left. (Courtesy of the author.)

Old Bedlam, built in 1849, is the oldest military building in Wyoming. The right side is restored as the bachelor officers' quarters in the 1850s. The left side is restored to its appearance as post headquarters in 1863–1864, when Lt. Col. William O. Collins commanded the fort. The room behind his office was the commanding officers' mess and doubled as a conference room. Collins and his wife, Catherine, lived on the second floor, now furnished as it was in 1864. (Courtesy of the author.)

The first building south of the surgeon's quarters on officers' row was a mixture of frame, adobe, concrete, and stone. It was built from an existing ordnance storehouse, gun shed, and powder magazine. All that is left of this building, which served as officers' quarters, is a portion of a concrete wall. (Courtesy of the author.)

The stone magazine has been restored to its mid-1800s appearance. The building held all of the post's weapons and ammunition, except the large field pieces. (Courtesy of the author.)

This was the house normally occupied by the post surgeon and his family. It was built in 1875 and was among the better quarters intended for higher-ranking officers. The Victorian furnishings reflect the surgeon's position as one of the cultural leaders of the military community. The south half of the duplex has been restored to its appearance as of 1880. (Courtesy of the author.)

Lt. Col. Andrew Burt, an officer in the 7th U.S. Infantry, was a respected soldier and Civil War veteran. Burt and his wife, Elizabeth, were stationed at Fort Laramie twice, the second time in 1887–1888, the period to which the interior of this house is restored and the period when the Burt family lived in the house. The Burts preferred furnishings that were relatively plain compared to the ornate décor in most of the other officers' homes. (Courtesy of the author.)

The post trader's store (Sutler's Store) was built in 1849 and was operated by a civilian licensed by the army. The store did a profitable business for 40 years with soldiers, Native Americans, gold seekers, and immigrants. The exterior of the store has been restored to its appearance in the 1880s. The north section served as the sutler's headquarters and, for a time, as the post office. (Courtesy of the author.)

The post trader's store supplied everything from staples and whiskey, to heavy tools and weapons. From its shelves, soldiers could supplement the bare necessities they were issued by the army, and civilians could purchase supplies. The interior of the store is restored to its appearance around 1865, and the shelves are stocked with items similar to those of the era. The counter top in this photograph is the original. (Courtesy of the author.)

An 1883 addition to the post trader's store housed the officers' club and a bar for enlisted men and civilians. The post trader provided the most readily accessible source of alcoholic beverages. The pool table shown here was the original pool table, weighing 3,000 pounds and brought by wagon to the fort in 1875. (Courtesy of the author.)

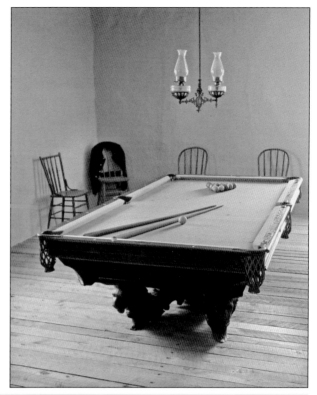

Mark Serour, an interpretive guide at Fort Laramie, poses behind the bar in the officers' club. Visitors today may purchase soft drinks such as sarsaparilla, cream soda, and birch bark soda at the bar. (Courtesy of the author.)

In the foreground of this photograph is a monument that was installed in 1913 to mark the historic location of Fort Laramie. Located northwest of the monument was the post trader's house. The house was built by the Ward-Bullock partnership, early post traders at Fort Laramie. All that is left of the ornate house (seen on page 63, as it looked in 1878) is the foundation. The cavalry barracks are in the background. (Courtesy of the author.)

The cavalry barracks was the largest building at Fort Laramie and the earliest of the lime-concrete structures to survive intact. It was built to meet the need for more housing during the Indian wars. Soldiers slept in two large, open squad bays on the second floor. Today the soldiers' rooms are furnished with authentic items of the day, including, uniforms, saddles, and weapons. The first sergeant had a private room downstairs. The mess hall downstairs is furnished to the way it appeared when soldiers were stationed at Fort Laramie. (Courtesy of the author.)

The hospital was built on the site of the old cemetery, which was used by the army until 1867. The ruins of the hospital remain today on the hillside at the northwest side of the fort. (Courtesy of the author.)

Old Bedlam, the jewel of the post, is all decked out for a celebration. Fort Laramie celebrated the 175th anniversary of the founding of Fort William with ceremonies between June 19 and 21, 2009. The program included a living history camp, formal presentations, and a special post office cancellation. (Courtesy of the author.)

BIBLIOGRAPHY

Brown, Larry K. *The Hog Ranches of Wyoming*. Glendo, WY: High Plains Press, 1995.

Griske, Michael. *The Diaries of John Hunton*. Westminster, MD: Heritage Books, Inc., 2005.

Hafen, LeRoy R., and Francis Marion Young. *Fort Laramie and the Pageant of the West*. Lincoln, NE: University of Nebraska Press, 1984.

Hieb, David L. *Fort Laramie*. Washington, D.C.: National Park Service Historical Handbook Series No. 20, 1954.

Larson, Robert W. *Red Cloud; Warrior-Statesman of the Lakota Sioux*. Norman, OK: University of Oklahoma Press, 1997.

Larson, T.A. *History of Wyoming*. Lincoln, NE: University of Nebraska Press, 1978.

McChristian, Douglas C. *Fort Laramie, Military Bastion of the High Plains*. Norman, OK: Arthur H. Clark Company, 2008.

Moulton, Candy. *Roadside History of Wyoming*. Missoula, MT: Mountain Press Publishing Company, 1995.

Unrau, William E. *Tending the Talking Wire*. Salt Lake City, Utah: University of Utah Press, 1979.

www.arcadiapublishing.com

Discover books about the town where you grew up, the cities where your friends and families live, the town where your parents met, or even that retirement spot you've been dreaming about. Our Web site provides history lovers with exclusive deals, advanced notification about new titles, e-mail alerts of author events, and much more.

MADE IN THE USA

Arcadia Publishing, the leading local history publisher in the United States, is committed to making history accessible and meaningful through publishing books that celebrate and preserve the heritage of America's people and places. Consistent with our mission to preserve history on a local level, this book was printed in South Carolina on American-made paper and manufactured entirely in the United States.

This book carries the accredited Forest Stewardship Council (FSC) label and is printed on 100 percent FSC-certified paper. Products carrying the FSC label are independently certified to assure consumers that they come from forests that are managed to meet the social, economic, and ecological needs of present and future generations.

FSC
Mixed Sources
Product group from well-managed forests and other controlled sources

Cert no. SW-COC-001530
www.fsc.org
© 1996 Forest Stewardship Council

Find Your Place in History.